PRINCIPLES OF MY FATHER
A MASTER TRIAL PRACTITIONER

By

Chris Lisle

In Memory of My Father, Whose Principles Guided Me Both Yesterday and Today

My Father and Me, about 1992

FOREWORD

I was born and raised in a small town, raised by an attorney/father I liken to Atticus Finch, with whom I would later practice law. At every stage of my life, even as a small boy, I was in his office playing or watching him try cases. In First Grade, I remember expressing an opinion and him inquiring of me, "How are you going to prove that?" He never released me from the mental hold of that question, not even after I became a lawyer. I know now that it was more than a question, and that he wasn't simply being adversarial or dismissive of what I thought, he was trying to instill in me a way of thinking, of coming to my own truth; it was a lifelong lesson on the burden of proof from a Master Practitioner.

My Father was a Master Trial Practitioner, meaning a great trial lawyer who achieved great results because he mastered the three pillars of ethics, technical skills, and common sense that all great trial Masters acquire. This "Principles of the Master Practitioner" are the lessons I learned from him and from the many other Master Practitioners I had the honor of working with or against along the way. Though I never became a Master, you just might.

Table of Contents

Principles of the Master Practitioner . . . 6

The Verdict . . . 8

Lessons of the Verdict . . . 16

Horatius Cocles . . . 18

On Ethics, the end doesn't justify the means . . . 20

Trial Reputations are earned by winning, not losing . . . 22

What is a Good Lawyer? . . . 22

You are the Face of Your Client . . . 23

Focus on your heart and not tripping on your words . . . 23

The importance of your client . . . 23

Be Decisive . . . 24

People are persuaded by stories, not logic . . . 24

Factless opinions are worthless . . . 27

If you can't say it in twenty words or less, you don't know what you're talking about . . . 28

Who is telling the truth? . . . 29

Voir Dire . . . 32

Opening Statement . . . 41

The Calling of Witnesses . . . 43

The Danger of "I don't know" . . . 45

Cross Examination a real life example . . . 47

Cross Examination in General . . . 54

Don't forget to elicit the magic words for your expert's opinion . . . 55

Closing Argument . . . 56

Epilogue – The Killing of Billy Holley . . . 60

About the Author . . . 67

*****

Principles of a Master Trial Practitioner

Be ethical. No case or client is worth your career or reputation. Whether you win or lose, always shake hands when it's over.

Above all else, use common sense.

Begin each case by drafting your closing argument. This is your theme, the end result you seek. Knowing where you want to go will direct your path through pleadings and discovery, and with each witness during the trial.

Don't wait for court deadlines to draft the key jury instructions. Prepare them at the beginning of your case so that you never go astray.

Be a strategist. All trials involve strategy from filing the initial pleading to delivering the closing argument. Don't fight over every issue. Learn which issues to fight and which to strategically concede and avoid suffering pyrrhic victories.

"Chance favors the prepared mind" Louis Pasteur. Chance is a factor in trial; eliminate the factor of chance with thorough preparation. Avoid preparing your opponent by filing needless discovery and motions. Every time you force your opponent to think about the case, they get better.

Be technically and tactically proficient. Know the rules of evidence and procedure. Master the art of direct and cross-examination. Know how to tactically object and overcome objections at trial.

You reap what you sow. Professional karma is real and will come back to haunt you in this trial and the next. Be fair and honest with opposing counsel in everything you do.

"No matter how good you are, never let them see you coming" from the Devil's Advocate. Never make your opponent mad, or they will work harder to beat you. Use kindness to your advantage and allow them

to focus on their other cases, not yours. Let them consider you the easy target, and surprise them in the courtroom.

Judges have long memories – never lie to a judge, they won't forget, ever.

Don't exaggerate, the jury won't forgive you and shouldn't.

Don't scream and shout. If the law is on your side, the lawyer argues the law. If the facts are on your side, the lawyer argues the facts. If neither are on your side, the lawyer will scream, shout and bang on the table. If your opponent is screaming and shouting, that's a good sign. If you are, it's not. Results speak louder than you can shout. Let your results speak for themselves. Threaten nothing.

Trial reputations are earned by winning, not losing, so pick your battles wisely, or your reputation will suffer and so will your pocket book.

*****

The Verdict

There is sacredness in tears. They are not the mark of weakness, but of power.

Washington Irving

A law professor once asked our class if courtrooms deliver justice. I already knew the answer. I learned it watching my Father try a case when I was still a boy. I learned it sitting on a hard wooden bench at the old Fayetteville Courthouse, watching my Father deliver his closing argument to twelve jurors in a case he called the "Pap" case.

When I was ten years old, my Father took me to the old Fayetteville courthouse for a trial he was finishing. We entered the courthouse through the basement door. Down in the basement, hanging on the wall, was a big mural, a painting of soldiers, sailors and Marines of past wars. Across the top of the mural was a saying "Our Hope lies in Heroic Men."

Over the many years, many lawyers had entered this courthouse through the same basement doors and passed by this same mural on their way upstairs to the courtroom to do battle. My Father was one of them. I never forgot that old mural, and often wondered if it affected my Father like it affected me.

As we passed the mural, I saw the elevator, but we didn't take it, we took the stairs. Taking the stairs didn't surprise me, though, for my

Father had a saying "why sit when you can stand, why walk when you can run." Though his saying didn't mention anything about stairs or elevators, I knew if we weren't supposed to sit or walk, we wouldn't be taking the elevator either.

When we got into the courtroom, my Father sat me on a hard wooden bench where visitors were allowed to sit and watch. I sat on the bench behind my Father. My Father sat with his clients at a table not far from the jury. My Father represented a mom and Father who had lost all three sons. I don't remember the parents' names.

My Father didn't have to tell me to be quiet, for neither of us had said a word since we entered the old courthouse. From the moment we entered the old courthouse and passed the mural, I could see the gravity of the situation written all over his face. He was deep in thought, and I knew better than to disturb him.

I was alone in the visitor section. I don't know why my brothers and mom weren't there or why I wasn't in school. If I had been sick, I'm sure I would have been at home with my mom, but I wasn't. At the time, it didn't seem unusual to be there alone, in fact, I was excited to be there, but now, I wish I knew why.

Not long before my Father died of dementia, I asked him why he took me. I asked because even though he had dementia, sometimes people with dementia vividly recall pieces of their past. Unfortunately, when I asked about the Pap case all he could say was "that was terrible."

Pap was a slum lord who refused to replace a faulty floor heater in a little wooden tinder box of a house. The heater was the sole source of heat in the little house. One cold winter night, that faulty heater started a fire. The house burned to the ground before the fire department could get there, and before the three boys could get out. The fire department found their charred bodies cuddling each other in a corner of the bedroom that they shared. The fire department or police took a picture of them as they found them. Mr. Pap told the fire department that he didn't understand why the dog could get out but the boys couldn't.

In law school, my Father told me that there were only two types of lawyers, those that help the big guy and those that help the little guy. He said that after law school each lawyer had to choose a side and so would I. He said that thirty years ago, he chose to help the little guy like his Father, a poor chicken farmer. But he said there wasn't much money in it.

Pap was the big guy in this case. He was the guy that chose to pinch a few pennies and not replace a faulty space heater he had repeatedly been asked to replace. Pap never did, and instead of asking himself why he didn't replace the heater, he faulted instead three little boys for not being able to get out of a burning house when the dog could.

Then my Father got up to make his closing argument. Watching my Father, the jury and the judge was like watching Atticus Finch in my favorite movie "To Kill a Mockingbird." "To Kill a Mockingbird" was about a poor country lawyer named Atticus Finch who defended a black man falsely accused of a rape. Like Atticus, my Father was a poor country lawyer, and like Scout and her brother watching their Father Atticus try his case, I was watching my Father try his.

My Father told the jury that if they thought Pap was at fault, they would then have to try and place a monetary value on the lives of those three little boys, but how could a price ever be put on the lives of those three little boys or any child? It's something my Father said would be difficult to do and that, despite what the law might suggest, there's no mathematical formula for doing it. He said the law didn't have a mathematical formula for placing a value on the life of a child, but that the law allowed them to deduct from whatever value they came up with the cost of raising that child (that law has since been changed, but at that time, it was the law).

My Father said the law allowing the deduction of expenses for raising a child simply didn't make sense, and thankfully the jury would also be told to use their common sense. And common sense said no parent dreams of having and raising children for any type of monetary gain. If parents only had kids for economic benefit, they wouldn't have them because it wouldn't make any economic sense. So, if there was no economic benefit to having children, why did people keep having them? Why do married couples dream of having kids and why, then, when a child is lost, or when three boys die in a fire, do their parents cry?

Anyone who would measure the life of the child by how much money they could make off of that child never loved a child of their own and would be incapable of crying at their funeral. With that, my Father looked at Pap.

"The parents of these three boys cried then and they cry today and would gladly pay any figure you could come up with if, by paying your award, they could have them back. But they will never have them back and no amount of money will ever heal the broken hearts of a mother and father who have lost all their children."

Then, I saw my Father cry. He was ashamed by his lack of composure and looked down. What he didn't see when he looked down, was that the old farmer sitting on the jury, sitting just in front of him, started crying too.

Eventually, all was said. The lawyers sat down and the jury "retired" to the back room to make their decision.

While they were out, I went to the table where my Father had been sitting to see the fire department photo. My Father had blown it up to poster size for the jury to see, but I couldn't see it from where I sat. It was lying against other exhibits, and now that the trial was over, I wanted to see it. While he talked to his clients, I went over to look at it. When he saw me put my hand on it, he put his hand on my own and stopped me. He didn't want me to see that photo. Our eyes met, and though we still hadn't talked since we came through the basement door, our eyes spoke now and I asked him please. He let go my hand and I looked at the photo.

The three boys in the photo were charred black beyond recognition. They were so badly burned that none of them had facial features, no fingers or toes. They looked like boys carved out of charcoal. Their arms clung to one another, showing that in the last moments of their precious little lives, they loved one another dearly. It made me think of my two brothers and me. They were probably about the same ages as us. I believe it reminded my Father of us too, and I've always wondered if that's why I was in the courtroom that day, to remind him of why he was there.

Not long after, the jury knocked on the door and came back with their verdict. At that time, it was the largest jury award for the death of a child in Arkansas.

So, to answer the professor's question, do courtrooms deliver justice? The answer is no. The Pap verdict didn't change anyone's heart, not Pap's or the parents, and didn't bring those boys back to life. Pap walked out of that courtroom as mean and miserly as he walked in, and that jury award didn't heal the broken hearts of the grieving parents. The boys never came home.

But I did see justice in the courtroom that day, in the heart and tears of my Father who pursued justice against Mr. Pap for the lives of three little boys lost forever, in hope that next time, Mr. Pap might fix a heater if for no reason than to prevent himself from being sued.

As the mural on the courthouse wall says, our hope lies in the heroic men and women who fight for it, and that "terrible" day as my

Father would later call it, and that memory of the mural and my Father in the courtroom, are forever sketched in my mind.

*****

Lessons of the Verdict

What I didn't realize sitting in that courtroom so many years ago, and didn't realize until many years later, was the value of a powerful story with a cause to root out evil in the community. Everything I ever needed to know about being a lawyer and trying a case I witnessed that day – watching a master trial attorney tell a powerful story of a modern "Scrooge." It's an old story which has stood the test of time for good reason. It is the story of a man who buried himself under a pile of gold and suffocated all life out of himself. Inherent in the story of Scrooge is that life is priceless, especially the lives of children.

It would have been a moral crime for my Father to have asked the jury for a specific dollar amount for the lives of those children and he didn't. It would have been a hypocrisy with no bounds to argue that children are priceless and then turn around and put a price on their heads, but it's hard for a lawyer not to ask for money, because that's what they are standing on the bridge fighting for - compensation. It took courage to hold strong in his personal belief that children were too priceless for a lawyer to come up with a figure, so only the jury would have to, because he couldn't, as evidenced by his tears. And the jury cried with him.

Though my Father never asked the jury to punish Pap, he didn't have to. Juries get it. They knew no award would assuage the tears of the grieving parents and inferred that the real reason for a high award was to punish this local Scrooge. My Father always cautioned me about asking for punitive damages, for you risk the jury thinking you're greedy. He said that if the facts justify it, the jury will know and award it in a higher compensatory award, maybe add to the pain and suffering of your client.

*****

Horatius Cocles

Horatius was a famous Roman Soldier, famous because he courageously stood on a narrow bridge and prevented a larger enemy force from crossing into Rome. All of Horatius' comrades ran. They ran before the fight even began. They ran because they saw they were outnumbered. Fear took hold and they fled. Horatius stood and fought because he picked his place of battle, the bridge, where he knew they had to fight him one on one. He trusted his skills and knew that he could hold out, and so can you.

The trial attorney is the modern Horatius and the courtroom is the bridge where you choose to stand and fight. No matter how big your opponent nor how big the law firm opposing you, your opponent cannot bring all their attorneys or resources to fight at the same time. This isn't a gang fight, this is a courtroom, where only one lawyer is allowed to speak at a time, through one witness at a time, and one of those lawyers speaking will be you. You will be given just as much time to speak as your opponents.

On paper, Horatius was out numbered, but on the bridge the odds were evened out. The same is true in the courtroom. Even if the other firm is bigger than yours, they can only fight you one at a time. In fact, smaller is bigger in the courtroom. On the day of trial, large law firms make a point of trying to appear, to a jury, to be much smaller and meeker than they are. Common sense says size matters in a courtroom so big firms try to avoid the classic "David and Goliath" fight, for juries are sympathetic to the underdog. But to the practitioner, have confidence that size doesn't matter in court and neither do race, gender, ethnicity, or how tall or how fat you are. The courtroom is the great equalizer; it is the bridge where Horatius fought, and all you need is the courage and skill of Horatius.

*****

On Ethics, the End Doesn't Justify the Means.

A warrior knows that the ends do not justify the means. For there are no ends, there are only means.
Paulo Coelho

Alexander Hamilton said "**The first duty of society is justice.**" Our justice system can be no more "just" than the attorneys who profess to honor and adhere to it. The definition of "justice" is fairness, moral rightness. Professional ethics are the foundation of the justice system, the means of fairness and morality moving us towards the "just" end we seek. The rules of evidence and civil procedure both assume the ethical candor of the lawyer, and are rendered meaningless without ethics, which are the means as to how we practice our profession.

But isn't all fair in love and war? Aren't we Horatius fighting the just cause on the bridge? Even war has ethics, there are such things as war crimes, but people often fall victim to the fallacy that the end justifies the means, it doesn't. The end justifying the means is a fallacy built on the false assumption that an immoral means can somehow produce a moral result. It can't. For example, if one wants to make a lot of money, does that "end" goal of making money justify stealing? No. If one believes in justice, does that justify killing the accused without a trial? No. Does the end ever justify an attorney lying to a client, the court, or peers, of withholding or destroying evidence, or tampering with witnesses? No. Thus, there is a flaw in the question "Does the end justifies the means?" for it falsely assumes the end can somehow sanctify the way we got there - even if it was immoral. It can't, not if it is to be a moral end, and our system of justice seeks a moral end.

The "end" goal of morality and fairness and the "means" by which we practice the profession become one. If justice is the foundation of our society, then we must adhere to the Code of Ethics in all that we do. There can be no greater justice than in how attorneys choose to practice it.

After my Father's death, these words were found penciled on notes he kept from a speech given to Junior High Students.

"If you truly work for other people, your community, and your country, these in turn will recognize you and honor you for it. This is the only true honor and is the only recognition worth having. You will be recognized not because you demand it; not because you deserve it; but because those you worked for want to honor you."

*****

Trial Reputations are Earned by Winning, not by Losing

Reputations are earned by winning, not losing. Trial attorneys are no different than any other profession be it football, boxing, or war. If you cannot win, people won't feel threatened when you threaten to go to court. The only reputation you get from losing is a reputation for losing. So, be smart when picking cases to try. Not all cases prove to be winners. Poor facts make poor law meaning it is a poor case to try. Horatius won, because he fought on a narrow bridge he knew he could hold and knew he had the skill to fight.

What is a Good Lawyer?

I find little difference between a good mother and a good lawyer. As children we ran to our mothers, as adults we run to our lawyers. A great lawyer is always a great mother. We run to either depending on where we are in life, and whichever one we run to, the best of the best are always glad to see us, always listens, exercises great patience to calm us in our hour of need, offers sage advice, corrects us when they must, and fights for us when we can't. A good lawyer is always a good mother. And a good mother is always a good lawyer.

You are the Face of Your Client

It's hard for a jury to like your client if they don't like you. You are literally the face of your client, the door to your client's cause. You are the first and last voice a jury will hear. Your reputation with the jury starts in voir dire, follows you into the parking lot during breaks, the bathroom, and won't end until the jury returns a verdict and goes home. Never forget that the jury is always watching you and act accordingly.

Focus on your Heart and not Tripping on Your Words

If jurors believe you are authentic, they are forgiving of how you say it. Research shows that communication is 60% visual, about 30% tone of voice, and 10% choice of words. That's a good thing. This means that people, aka juries, are not "grammar Nazis", if you stumble over your words they will forgive you if they believe in you.

The Importance of Your Client

During a quiet moment at a mediation of a high stakes case, a great national trial lawyer privately confided that **"I could have won every case I ever tried if my client didn't have to testify."** No truer words have ever been said. This is the secret fear of every trial lawyer, that their client will betray the great story they just told the jury. There is no more important witness than your client. The law is so general that if the jury likes your client, they can find for them. If they don't like them, they can find against them.

Be Decisive

Lawyers must be decisive in trial. Voltaire said that **perfection is the enemy of good**, and this is true in the courtroom, for there is no time for perfect decisions when forced to think on your feet. "Quick wit" has more to do with experience than it does mental agility. After one hundred jury trials, there is little that a witness can say or opposing counsel can do that the veteran lawyer hasn't seen, so what may seem like quick wit is really experience coming to bear; so younger lawyers must focus on preparation to overcome experience, but young or old, trial attorneys must be decisive by remembering there is no right or wrong decision, only the best decision to be made with the information available. Be decisive.

People are Persuaded by Stories, not Logic.

Research confirms people learn through stories, not by logical deduction. Growing up, we hear, ad nauseam, family stories: stories of grandparents, parents, relatives and friends. We are read children stories, fables, we go to movies, and quotes from movies instill into our vernacular. We are fascinated with learning our history and with reality shows - all of these things fill our lives with metaphors and analogies, the springboard to learning. If it's analogous to our own lives, it must be true, for we know it to be true. Great trial lawyers tell a great story, a story that jurors relate to, have heard before, and are not a lesson in logic. Tell your client's story and relate it to the jury.

All stories consist of character, conflict and resolution. The characters are the plaintiff and defendant (one of whom is the protagonist), the conflict is the liability, and resolution is left for the jury to decide how that story will end. Most great trial lawyers have moral themes they use in every case, in every voir dire, opening, with every witness and in closing. In personal injury cases defense counsel will weave everything into the story of greed, of a plaintiff desiring something for nothing. With plaintiff's counsel, it will be the story of David vs. Goliath, or manifest injustice that only the jury can rectify or it will happen to them. So, what is the moral of the story that you want the jury to stamp on the verdict form?

Was It Murder or Self-Defense?

Billy lived with his younger brother in a small house they inherited from their mother. Billy didn't make much money, and the money he did make he spent it all on beer. Billy drank because he wasn't happy, and he would drink all night trying to forget his problems – but his biggest problem, the one he couldn't let go of, was the bottle in his hand. He was an angry drunk, drunk and angry most of the time.

One Friday night, Billy and his younger brother had a friend visiting. As Billy got tanked up, he became unusually angry. His friend left before the anger got worse, but his younger brother could not. We know from the records that Billy's blood alcohol level was .028, an alcohol level only possible in the most extreme alcoholics. That night, Billy's anger gave way to the usual bullying of his younger brother, and the bullying turned into a fight. This wasn't the first fight, for Billy often beat his younger brother. Billy attacked his brother in the kitchen. The younger brother grabbed a small pocket knife, the kind you can buy at any local store, and poked it forward to keep Billy away from him. Billy got poked one time, just above the belly button. The cut was less than an inch deep, but just so happened to nick Billy's aorta.

Billy immediately fell to the ground. His brother dropped the knife and immediately called the ambulance. The ambulance got there within five minutes, but Billy was already dead, but Billy wasn't the victim that night. His younger brother was, and always had been. The friend that left early will testify to that, and testify that he left early because he was scared of Billy.

Factless opinions are worthless in or out of the courtroom.

The problem is, by the time lawyers get to court, they are busting at the seams to cry out "They are guilty!" or "They are liable!" Those are meaningless opinions to jurors who know nothing about the facts of the case and will rightly reject them. In opening, tell a factual story that drives a conclusion. For example, in opening, don't say "The man was speeding" but do say "The man was driving 50mph in a 25mph school zone." When questioning witnesses, don't argue (state your opinion), for a witness will argue back. Instead, elicit facts that draw the conclusions you want. For example, don't ask "Were you speeding?" or argue "You were speeding weren't you!" ask instead, "How fast were you going?"

At the end of the day, the only opinion that matters is the jury's. So, how do you get them to agree with yours? Remember, your opinion was based on a fact investigation. If your opinion was reasonably derived from the facts, parse out the credible facts important to your conclusion and regurgitate them to the jury in a story that they can understand and believe, a story that will be proved through the witnesses that testify. Like a movie, your opening is the preview of what they will hear. If you say it in opening, you better be able to back it up during trial with witnesses or suffer your credibility.

If you can't say it in twenty words or less, you don't know what you're talking about

Though "twenty words or less" may be a bit simplistic, the point is this: **no one likes the sound of your voice as much as you do**. Like the opening scene of a good movie, you have about twenty seconds to capture the jurors' imagination. In a crib death case, you might open with something like this:

> "Twelve month old Ann slept all night for the first time on October 1, 2010, but when her mom went to check on her the next morning, she found Ann wasn't sleeping at all. Sometime during the night, little Ann's crib had collapsed suffocating her. Despite the baby room monitors, her mom never heard little Ann cry, but her Mom has cried ever since."

This simple story only uses facts to quickly introduce the jury to a product liability claim (defective crib), pain and suffering of a mother (who has lost an infant), and thwart a claim of comparative fault (never heard her cry).

Who is telling the truth?

Jurors are given a seemingly impossible task to determine who is telling the truth. Every jury in this country is told to assess the credibility of the witnesses to pick out who's lying. Jurors expect a witness to testify favorably for their cause but is that person telling the truth? If not, why not? Most witnesses aren't liars and calling a witness a liar should be done sparingly and with caution, less you be made the fool. Good lawyers rarely resort to this tactic. It is far better for the jury to come to this conclusion on their own through your effective direct and cross examination which proves bias or lack of knowledge.

So, how do you explain to a jury why all witnesses don't agree? William Faulkner said it best, **no one person has a claim to the truth, but each person carries a piece of it with them**. Trials are like life, no one witness has the whole truth of the case, but each person has a piece of it. If any one witness had the whole truth, it would be a one witness trial, but they never are.

The truth of each witness' testimony is limited by either lack of personal knowledge, or bias. Every witness has some bias or limitation and it is your job to bring that out. The doctor's testimony is limited by their area of expertise and what they examined. Friends and neutral witnesses are always limited in what they know or don't know and carry certain biases. Even the plaintiff can't testify about all their damages, take future medical expenses, for example, that requires an expert. The attorney's role is to honestly guide the jury through this process of separating truth from fiction, separating fact from opinion, separating opinion from conjecture, and start that process in opening, continue it in direct and cross examination, and finally sum it up in closing.

Some examples of how this can be approached in the opening–

The General Credibility of Witnesses

At the end of this trial, the judge will tell you that you must determine the credibility of the witnesses. Nothing is more important than determining what is true and what isn't. A trial is a process of trying to figure out the truth, where you listen to the witnesses and put it all together at the end to figure out what is the truth in this case. It's not as simple as it seems. A famous writer once said that no one person knows all the truth, but we each know a part of it. And, that's what a trial is. All of the witnesses you will hear have a piece of the truth, but none of them have all of it. If they did, it would be a one witness case, but it's not. This case involves multiple witnesses and will take many days, and as each person testifies you will have to decide which part of what they have to say is true and which is misplaced. It's not that they are intentionally lying, for most people are here to tell the truth, but each of them is limited by what they don't know, or maybe affected by their own personal biases because they are friends or family, or maybe limited by their physical point of view, where they were standing and what they could see, how long they had to see it, the lighting when they saw it, how long it's been since they saw it – for people are forgetful. At the end of this trial, you then must cipher through the witnesses, the conflicting testimony, and use the most reliable facts to come to the truth.

Credibility in the Battle of the Experts

Each side hired an expert. The fact that each side hired an expert who supports their side should be no surprise, for what attorney in their right mind would hire an expert that testifies for the other side? So, in this battle of the experts, who is telling the truth? Maybe this case doesn't need an expert. Maybe it only needs common sense to decide.

Credibility in a Case of Fraud

The defendant isn't going to take the stand and admit he defrauded my client. If he would, we wouldn't be here today, but he hasn't and he won't. This isn't a movie where the defendant breaks down on the stand and admits the truth. He's going to take the stand and tell you the same fraudulent thing he told my client, that he didn't know. The problem with people who defraud others is they sound and look believable, and those lies will sound just as believable to you as they did my client, and that's what we call fraud. And since he won't admit his fraud, we will prove it with "circumstantial evidence," which means we will allow him to repeat his lies and then use other evidence to prove the truth which he is unwilling to confess.

VOIR DIRE

Voir dire is critical and maybe the most critical point of a trial so spend time preparing and doing it well. There are studies which show at least half the jurors have made up their mind about the case by the time voir dire is done. How is that possible? It's only possible because jurors either like one lawyer better than another or if jurors have inherent biases, or it may be a combination of the two. So, to win in voir dire, you must establish your credibility and elicit and remove, if possible, jurors with inherent biases against your case.

How much time do you have to ask questions? How much time will the judge allow for voir dire? Federal Court is more limited than state courts, but in any court, how much time you have will determine how many questions you can ask and thus you can triage the questions most needed to be asked. Don't wait until the day of trial to find out how much time you will be given, because you won't have time to prepare your questions. During scheduling conferences or pre-trial conferences, ask how much time you will be given and how many peremptory challenges you will have. Don't assume, always ask, and always ask the judge, not your peers.

Research the list of jurors. Some courts have the list of jurors they will call. If they do, get it as soon as possible and start researching the jurors on social media and other public records to learn their biases and put you in a position to ask more directed questions.

Establish your credibility. Remember first and foremost, that you are the face of your client and your credibility is being established long before you start speaking. Watch your mannerisms and your tone of voice.

Know your opponent. Remember the principle of preparation? That preparation is key? Sun Tzu said if you know the enemy and know yourself, you need not fear 100 battles. So, know your enemy by watching them in court if possible. Coaches watch game tape of other teams all the time. You do the same. Either watch physically or read the transcript of a previous trial, but "knowing your enemy" is an old principle of war. See how your opponent conducts voir dire as it will probably be the same in each case. Go watch your opponent do an opening, it will be the same in almost all cases because great trial lawyers have big themes they always push – plaintiff's push "David vs. Goliath" and defendants "Plaintiff is greedy and wants something for nothing." Watch what your opponents do so you will be prepared to object or counter their themes. The famous lawyer Clarence Darrow once said his success in the courtroom was built over time based upon what worked for him in trial. If it worked, he kept doing it. If it didn't, he stopped. Most great trial lawyers are the same and develop habits, meaning their voir dire is similar if not the same from case to case. So, if you are going to try a case against "Clarence Darrow" take the time to go watch them in court.

The two philosophies for conducting voir dire: (1) use questions to tell your story (theme) or (2) use questions to elicit jurors with strong biases against your case – basically, do the jurors lean towards a plaintiff or defendant? If given time, Masters like to focus on eliciting juror biases if given time to inquire and trying to strike them from the jury.

I once had a wonderful conversation with a Master Trial Attorney with well over 100 jury trials. He works almost exclusively for the defense representing large corporations. I asked for his philosophy on voir dire and here are some of his replies:

I'm just not convinced that going into aggressive lawyering mode from the start works for the defense. There are lots of movies where the hero is a lawyer who takes on a large corporation and wins a big verdict for his client. There are virtually no movies where the hero is the corporate mouthpiece who shuts down the little guy. Jurors are familiar with the crusading Plaintiffs lawyer trope—not the sanctimonious defense lawyer. I've also been told that I look like a Central Casting stock character for the corporate defense lawyer, so I am trying from the beginning to get the jurors to view me as a person, and member of their community—not the corporate defense lawyer.

My strategy on voir dire is to identify jurors who are most likely to hurt my case so that they don't get sat. This means that I am generally asking questions that prompt responses from panel members who don't like big corporations or folks who are comfortable with the idea of lawsuits and claims. I want to exclude them for cause and save my preemptories for the ones that just give me a bad feel. My questions are more like this:

> *Does anybody think that corporations have too much power and influence over our government and policies?*

> *Does anybody think large corporations need to be more closely regulated and controlled to prevent abuses and protect individual rights?*

> *Does anybody think that individuals' rights to hold corporations or large institutions accountable need to be expanded by the courts or legislature?*

> *Does anybody feel that this company pays its workers unfairly or that it doesn't pay enough to hire high quality workers who care about safety?*

> *Does anybody feel that corporations like the company places more value on profits than customer safety?*

> *Does anybody think that organized labor needs to become stronger to counter the power and influence of large corporations?*

> *Does anybody have any objection to the way that The company does business?*

> *Would anybody have strong feelings if a big company moved into your community or neighborhood?*

And then I ask questions about whether they or someone
close to them has ever filed a lawsuit, claim, etc.

If they answer yes to any of those questions, I am going to try and get them off for cause or get them to admit that their feelings could affect their verdict or make them less favorable to my client. I usually don't ask all of these questions; but even a few will prompt some responses and identify the bad jurors.

Some trial lawyers would say that I am seeding the room with bad ideas about corporations; and that some prospective jurors might be influenced by what these pro-plaintiff's jurors say in a public room. But I want to identify both those types. The types that hold these ideas that are hostile to my client; and the types that could become influenced easily by some negative opinion that another juror holds. At the same time, I want jurors that feel that there are too many lawsuits, favor tort reform, or place a premium on personal responsibility to shut up and say nothing during voir dire, because I don't want the Plaintiff's lawyer to be able to easily identify and exclude them. So, I don't push any of those questions; and I wouldn't point out that anybody can file a lawsuit for $200; or suggest that lawsuits are a bad thing—in voir dire. In fact, I would want to identify anybody who thinks it's great that you can sue a company simply by paying $200.

Now, there is another school of thought that suggests that your opening statement starts in voir dire; and you should be seeding the room with your themes before the trial even starts. I have heard their viewpoint; and think that it might lull them into a false sense that the jurors are predisposed to them. In my opinion, jurors are suspicious and wary during voir dire and they are not open to being persuaded because you have not earned their trust. In my voir dire, I will start with that idea:

Folks, we just met; and I would not presume to think that I
earned your confidence or trust to begin telling you how I
think you should feel about this case, lawsuits in general,
or corporations like my client. Instead, this is the only
opportunity that I will have before any verdict is

announced in this case to learn how you feel about certain issues which might be important in deciding whether this is the best case for you to sit. We've all been on this earth long enough to have our own experiences and develop our own opinions. They are your own experiences and opinions; and there are no right or wrong answers to the questions I will be asking. The legal process only works if the participants are honest and candid; and throughout this trial you will expect the witnesses to be honest and truthful in answering any questions they are asked. I am going to trust that you will hold yourself to the same standard and be just as honest and candid in answering these questions, which will help decide whether this is the best case for you to sit on; or whether there might be a case or matter that better suits you somewhere else in this courthouse.

That's not verbatim, but it's pretty close in venues where we are allowed more leeway to conduct voir dire. In other venues, we are much more limited, and I might only get the judge to ask a question like: "Does anybody have strong feelings, good or bad, about companies like the company?" Or, "are you or any family members, involved in a union or affiliated with a union."

I am very careful about trying to imply that a complaint is fraudulent or frivolous.

Each side should ask questions on burden of proof, proximate cause and general biases about how jurors feel about the filing lawsuits, how they feel about awarding big damages, and punitive damages, or in criminal cases, do they assume a person is guilty because they have been charged? Many times, jurors will be asked what news sources they like to help glean whether they are conservative or liberal.

Identify the strong jurors. As a general rule, attorneys try to identify strong personalities, as those potential jurors will likely be the foreperson and a strong advocate in the jury room. If you don't know which way this person leans, you will want to try and strike them for cause or use a peremptory challenge. Remember the principle to be fair? If you are worried about how they lean, the other side is probably worried too, and you may be able to get a joint agreement to strike the person for cause. An example of a strong juror would be one who has expertise in a field that is at issue in the trial, for these are going to be "strong" jurors that will potentially second guess your expert. An example would be a doctor as a juror on a case involving medical testimony, a carpenter on a construction case, an accountant or a business evaluation case, etc. Always ask who has served on a jury and if they have served, if they were the foreperson. People who have served on juries will be stronger jurors in your case.

Preparation is key, research jurors if you can, and plan your questions around important themes or issues in your case. If the case involves an issue like alcohol, you have to ask questions about how people feel about alcohol. Always inquire on the issue of burden of proof and proximate cause.

The battle for early credibility is often initiated in voir dire, and usually over the "Burden of Proof." Plaintiff's counsel will or should attempt to define the "burden of proof" and then use an analogy to explain it to the jury. Common analogies are "the scales of justice" tipping ever so slightly to their side or maybe "fifty one pieces of paper vs. fifty pieces of paper", or maybe they don't have to cross the goal line only the "fifty-one yard line," but no matter the analogy given of meeting the burden of proof, it is likely to draw an objection, an objection that the burden of proof was improperly defined, and that the definition of burden of proof is for the judge and not counsel.

Whether you are plaintiff or defense counsel, be prepared to object or fight an objection. Objecting early in voir dire is either the other attorney testing your ability to recover, or the other attorney is trying to impugn your credibility by suggesting you're not being fair, and certainly trying to take the early initiative in trial. No matter the reason, the battle for initiative and credibility is always important. Be prepared to object or to respond. Research the rules for voir dire, know what is proper and improper, know your adversary and how they conduct it and what they are likely to say or object to you saying. Never be visibly upset if you lose an objection! Jurors can't tell that you lost from "sustained."

Here are a few sample questions plaintiff's counsel may ask in a civil trial for damages to elicit jurors who are pro defendant:

1. How do you feel about punitive damages?

2. How many people feel they are wrong?

3. How many people wouldn't award them even if the judge said that's the law?

4. How many people think there are too many lawsuits?

On the flip side, defense counsel might ask:

1. How many people have ever filed a personal injury suit?

2. How many people are or have been a member of a labor union?

Here are just a couple of questions defense lawyers in a civil trial will ask:

> (a) Thank you ladies and gentlemen. You will notice that the plaintiff asked questions first and then me. That process will be repeated throughout this trial. The plaintiff will go first and I will go last. The plaintiff will give his opening first and I will go second. The plaintiff will put their witnesses on first and mine will follow. Will you all please promise me that you will not decide this case until after I have a chance to put on my witnesses?

> (b) In this case, the judge and plaintiff will tell you that the plaintiff has the burden of proof. This means that I don't have to put on any witnesses. If I don't put on

any witnesses, would any of you find my client liable simply because they didn't put on any witnesses?

(c) If someone was in a car wreck told you that their car wreck caused their lung cancer, you probably wouldn't believe them. That's what we call proximate cause. You wouldn't believe the wreck was the proximate cause of her cancer. In this case, you will hear the plaintiff had a knee replacement was proximately caused by the fall. We will put on medical testimony that the knee replacement was not proximately caused by the fall. Will you keep your mind open about the cause of the injury until after I put on medical testimony about the cause of her knee replacement?

OPENING STATEMENT

How important is it? Some experts say that by now, after openings, up to 80% of jurors have made up their mind.

You need to tell a story, but here are helpful pointers to flesh it out and make critical facts more memorable. **Remember that people learn orally, visually, and physically meaning hands on**. Try to use all three in opening and throughout the case. All trials involve critical dates and records. These should be made "visually" as well to help the jury remember them and understand their significance as the trial plays out.

Simple time lines in an opening are good – for a written timeline adds "visual" allowing jurors to better mark important dates in their memories. For example, a personal injury should note the date of the accident, date released from treatment, or dates of pre-existing injuries and treatment if that is an issue.

Like adding a visual timeline, it's good to identify and exhibit a few of the critical and favorable records or other physical evidence to the flag these for their attention (if the judge allows). If the jury hears you say they are important and also sees them, it is more impressionable and they will be listening for them during the trial and have context for them.

Identifying key witnesses and explaining what they will say and why it's important is critical. If the judge allows, attorneys will sometimes play, in their opening, critical video deposition testimony.

Preparation is key! Be it theater, sports or politics, no one takes the stage without lots of dress rehearsals, so at a minimum, do a dress rehearsal of your opening. Videotape yourself doing your opening with all exhibits wearing whatever you plan to wear at trial. It's cheap and easy to do. What will you learn? Rarely do we look or make as much sense as we think we do. The video will keep you honest and allow you to make adjustments. Every other profession rehearses, lawyers rarely do. Only lawyers have the confidence to wing it, but only one person winging it gets to win.

If you're a defendant in a civil case, be cautious about impugning the plaintiff's claim by saying "anyone can file a claim for $200." It can come across wrong. Some jurors may have filed claims (and not disclosed it). Even if they haven't, they may take it the wrong way, plaintiff's counsel will use your words against you in closing.

The Calling of Witnesses

What is your burden of proof? If you have the burden of proof on any issue, then you will need a witness or witnesses to meet the elements of that burden. Know your jury instructions and then figure out which witnesses are needed to meet each element of that burden.

Remember, chance is a factor in all trials, so eliminate the risk of chance by only calling necessary witnesses. Before putting a witness on the stand, do a cost/benefit analysis and ask yourself what is the risk to my case presented by this witness? All witnesses present risk, some known and some unknown, so when deciding if you are going to call a witness do a cost/benefit analysis. If a witness isn't critical, meaning you have other witnesses or evidence to give evidence on the same point, it lessens your need to call that witness. Sometimes, you can use cross examination to get your opponent's witnesses to make the same point, but never rely on using your opponent's witnesses unless you have

secured that testimony in a deposition or form where you are sure you can get it into evidence at trial. At trial, if you opponent's witness makes your point, you may then decide not to call a risky witness waiting to take the stand, but make sure you are prepared at trial to meet your burden of proof.

Preparation of witnesses is key but can be difficult. It may be difficult because you can't always compel witnesses to talk to you before they take the stand to testify. But with your client, you have time to prepare, so prepare. Too many lawyers make the mistake of only preparing themselves and not enough time putting their client or witness through an effective simulation of a direct and cross examination. Too many lawyers only explain what will happen at court, go over the facts of the case, ask their witness to explain it, but this isn't enough. This soft ball style preparation only prepares the lawyer and isn't enough to prepare a witness who will be subject to a direct and cross examination.

When preparing a witness, you should put that witness through a simulated direct and cross examination to allow them to learn to answer questions under stress. Too many witnesses buckle under the pressure of trial or deposition. Most people have a desire to be cooperative and thus, when subject to a cross exam with a "harsh tone" of voice have a natural tendency to try and be cooperative and concede when they shouldn't.

Witnesses have to practice to learn to listen for questions with hidden assumptions or compound questions before saying "Yes" because they might be saying yes to one part of the question but in reality, not the other part. So, caution your client to be wary anytime your opponent begins by saying "Wouldn't you agree?" because they probably don't, not if they think about the question and understand what it is implying, not asking.

At trial, have a written checklist of key facts you need from each witness to insure you meet your burden of proof. Do not let that witness off the stand until you insure yourself that your check list is satisfied.

The Danger of "I don't know."

When a witness says "I don't know" it opens the door for the other side to run with it. Now, many times a witness must truthfully testify "I don't know" but as a trial lawyer, when you hear these words, either be prepared to shut the door or run through it and exploit the opportunity. In preparation of your own witnesses, try to know everything your witness knows and doesn't know so when they say "I don't know" you are prepared to deal with it at trial. At trial, be prepared to exploit when a witness says "I don't know."

Example:

Q: Did you have anything to drink that night?

A. Yes.

Q: How much did you drink?

A. I don't know.

Q. If you don't know, it could have been two beers?

A. Yes.

Q. If you don't know, it could have been a six pack couldn't it?

A. I don't think so.

Q. But you don't know do you?

A. No.

Q. So, if you don't know it could have been a six pack?

A. I guess.

Q. Since you don't know, you could have drank an entire case?

A. I don't know.

This is an example of a lawyer exploiting an "I don't know" and roughshodding a witness who capitulates because the witness wasn't adequately prepared.

Cross Examination, a Real Life Example

The Cross Examination of the Credible Mr. Reed

Cross examination is like fishing, always try to avoid being pulled into the water by your catch.

Louis Nizer

Mr. Reed was a former college football player. He was tall, dark, handsome, smart and charismatic. After college, he took all he learned in school along with his God given talents and became an appraiser, a very successful one.

Mr. Reed was as dangerous and charismatic in the field of appraising as he was on the gridiron. He quickly developed a reputation as an expert witness in the courtroom on land condemnation suits. No other appraiser could compete against the soft spoken charisma of Mr. Reed. If the numbers were in dispute, his innate charisma could be counted on to carry the day. It wasn't long before every government body condemning property hired Mr. Reed before a landowner could.

My Dad was a local attorney and longtime friend of Mr. Reed. Their friendship went back years and each shared a mutual respect and admiration for the other. But in the courtroom, my Dad had his job and Mr. Reed had his. Mr. Reed's job was to testify for the State and my

Dad's was to cross examine him on behalf of the landowner. My job? I was a young lawyer who had yet to ask a question in court. So my job was to sit and take notes. These are my notes.

When the State finished examining Mr. Reed, I was thoroughly convinced he was right. Had I been taken in by his charm? Maybe, but in the end it was all about the numbers and his added up in a way I could understand.

It was my Dad's turn to cross examine the credible Mr. Reed. My Dad had a habit of allowing a little time to pass before beginning his cross examination. Most people abhor the pressure of public speaking, but good trial attorneys must embrace it and cannot be distracted by the pressure of all the eyes studying their every move. A good trial attorney must enter that arena like they are fighting a bull and never take their eyes off the bull. My Dad stood before the credible Mr. Reed like a Matador. I didn't envy the position he was in, having to throw stones at this courtroom Goliath.

Where would my Dad begin? What would be his first question? How would he attack the credibility of a man he loved more than the jury? The surprise? He wouldn't, because it couldn't be done. What he would do instead is turn the credible Mr. Reed into a witness of his own.

Use the credible Mr. Reed to testify as to the credibility our meek, wobbly kneed expert appraiser, Mr. Smith. And by using Mr. Reed to testify to both the credibility and numbers used by Mr. Smith, he would cut off the other attorney's attack, because attacking Smith would essentially be attacking the opinion of their own witness, the credible Mr. Reed.

My Dad began:

Q: Mr. Reed, do you recognize the man sitting in the back of the courtroom (My Dad pointed to Mr. Smith)?

Mr. Reed: Yes.

Q: Who is he?

A: That's Mr. Smith.

Q: How do you know him?

A: I know him professionally, as an appraiser.

Q: How long have you known him?

A: At least fifteen years.

Q: Please describe the professional relationship you've had over those years?

A: During those years, we've served on various committees together.

Q: Was one of those committees the ethics committee?

A. Yes.

Q: Do you serve together on the ethics committee now?

A: Yes.

Q: What does the ethics committee do?

A: We investigate complaints that appraisers are not acting ethically in the way that they do appraisals.

Q: What is an example of that?

A: Sometimes there are complaints that an appraiser has not used proper comparable sales data or maybe not used a proper formula for calculating the value of a property.

Q: Has Mr. Smith ever had a complaint filed against him?

A: Not that I'm aware of.

Q: Are you aware that Mr. Smith did an appraisal of the property in this case?

A: Yes.

Q: Have you read that appraisal?

A. Yes.

Q: In this case, has anyone complained that Mr. Smith's appraisal violates the accepted methods for appraising property in the State of Arkansas?

A: No.

Q: Are you familiar with the comparable sales data used by Mr. Smith?

A: Yes.

Q: Are you also familiar with the formula Mr. Smith used to value this property?

A: Yes.

Q: Appraisers are allowed discretion when choosing comparable sales?

A: Some.

Q: And Mr. Smith's comparable sales are acceptable.

A. Yes but not the ones I would choose.

Q: Is there any suggestion that Mr. Smith's sales data is improper?

A: No.

Q: So the two of you, in picking sales data, properly used your discretion in picking comparable sales data?

A: Yes.

Q: And the properties used by both of you are acceptable under State of Arkansas appraisal standards?

A: Yes.

Q: Also Mr. Smith used a different formula to calculate value the property?

A: Yes.

Q: Mr. Smith's formula is an accepted valuation method?

A: Yes, but not the one I believe should be used.

Q: But it's an accepted method for valuing property that he has the discretion to use?

A: Yes.

Q: And the end result is that your formula gives a lower value than his?

A: Yes.

Q: So when you combine your sales data with your formula, it will always end up with a lower value than his sales data with his formula?

A: Yes.

Q: When you read Mr. Smith's appraisal and review the sales data with the formula he used, is his final number correct? Did his math add up?

A: Yes.

Q: No further questions for Mr. Reed.

Not once did my Dad attempt to cross examine the credible Mr. Reed on the values he used or the formula he used. That's a dangerous fight my Dad couldn't have won. Instead, he artfully used Mr. Reed's credibility to build the credibility of Mr. Smith. By using Mr. Reed's credibility instead of attacking it, it made it next to impossible for the other side to cross examine Mr. Smith, for Mr. Reed just told the jury that Mr. Smith was a credible appraiser he had known for fifteen years who properly used his discretion in this case.

The only question remaining for the jury was who's final number should they believe? Mr. Reed's or Mr. Smith's? By using the credibility of Mr. Reed to build the credibility of Mr. Smith, my Dad essentially put the two experts on par. Putting them on par shifted the issue of credibility from who had the most credible expert to who had the most credible attorney? It was now up to the attorneys to persuade the jurors whose number they should use.

After closing arguments, it didn't take long for the jury to return a verdict using Mr. Smith's number.

CROSS EXAMINATION IN GENERAL

In its simplest form, cross examination is either attacking a witness' credibility or buttressing your own by getting them to admit a fact or facts which help your case. **You can attack the witness by showing bias or lack of knowledge or try to get them to admit facts critical to your story**. It's not an either or proposition, for you can do both.

Although leading questions are allowed on cross, I find it more persuasive if the witness isn't "forced" into an answer but volunteers it. Here's an example:

> "You don't remember anyone cleaning up the spill." That could be asked more effectively "Do you remember anyone cleaning the spill?"

> Or

> "This was not the first time you had been to this home." That could be asked more effectively "Was this the first time you had been to this home?"

Don't forget to elicit the magic words for your expert's opinion

Never forget that your expert's opinion is worthless unless they use the magic words to get their opinion into evidence. **Each state will have a different standard or set of magic words to make their opinion admissible**, so know what the magic phrase is, otherwise your expert's opinion will be stricken and you've wasted a lot of time, money, and maybe lost your case. It seems simple right? But it's a technicality that trips many lawyers. Don't let it happen to you.

Some lawyers start with the golden question so they don't forget and so that the jury will know what the opinion is and thus have context for the facts that underlie it. This is probably the safest route if nothing else. How is this done? After qualifying the witness as an expert, you may then ask something like this:

> Q: "Dr. Jones, do you understand that I employed you form an opinion as to whether or not Ms. _____ 's knee replacement was caused by the car accident?"
> A: Yes.
> Q: Dr. Jones, have you formed an opinion as to whether Ms. _____ knee replacement was proximately caused by car accident?"
> A: I have.
> Q: Is that opinion within a reasonable degree of medical certainty (insert your magic phrase here)?
> Q: What is that opinion?

A: The accident was the proximate cause of the knee replacement.

Q: What was that opinion based upon?

A: Her medical records.

Q: What dates of her records did you review in coming to that opinion?

A: I reviewed from 2004 until present date.

Q: What in those records leads you to the opinion that her knee replacement wasn't caused by her fall?

A: She has a long history of arthritis that preceded the fall, and the knee replacement was the result of the pre-existing arthritis and not the car accident.

Starting with the opinion is only a technique, but, it does two things: (1) insures you don't forget to ask; (2) gets it out there while the jury is paying attention. They know quickly and immediately what the opinion is and then all information after that will be through that filter.

Closing Argument
Arming the Jurors

How important is it? Most jurors have already made up their mind, so you are arming favorable jurors with the arguments they will need to make when arguing your case in the jury room.

Master Attorneys begin mentally formulating "their closing" the first moment they get assigned a case. When a lawyer gets a case, they should immediately be thinking about their closing argument and how to get there. Everything in discovery should be tailored to proving that closing argument. In a criminal case, is it self-defense? Trial lawyers think and don't simply crank out the same stuff on each case like a factory worker working on the clock. Trying cases is like playing football games. Though Alabama has certain plays they like to run and themes for offense and defense, they don't play each game the same way. They study their opponent, think about the strengths and weakness of their opponent, and formulate a strategy to win next week's game based on the weaknesses of their opponent. Trial lawyers should do the same. Sure, we have common time tested themes, we have certain for voir dire, direct and cross examination, but each case is different the attorney must formulate an individual strategy exploiting the factual weakness of his opponent's case.

Like any good written story or speech, a trial should begin with a topic sentence (opening) and end on a conclusion (closing). The closing should essentially buttress your credibility by reminding the jury that in opening you told them "this" and the witnesses confirmed the truth of what you told them. If your opponent promised something in opening that wasn't delivered in trial, remind the jury of this.

In closing, many jurors will have made up their minds, so what you are trying to do is give those jurors who are on your side the arguments to take with them to the jury room and argue your case for you.

On the issue of closings, a great "Master" once told me:

I do have what is called my "wood pile" closing argument, which at least one judge has said in an opinion comes close to the line without crossing it. Here it is abbreviated:

> *Members of the jury, in the high country at one time, there was a code. Bad, life threatening weather can strike at any time, so hunters, trappers, and outdoors people left their sheds and cabins open, stocked, and unlocked. And they knew that there is this network of huts out there that can be reached if they are unlucky enough to get stuck outdoors and in need of shelter. The code was basic and there were only three rules: First, take only what you need. Second, if you have something to spare, leave it for the owner or the next person. And, third, and most importantly, always restock the wood pile. See, up in the high country or frontier, wood and fire means life; and when bad weather hits, there just isn't time to find and cut wood that can be burned or used to save a life. If folks don't restock the wood pile, then hut owners are going to be reluctant to leave their huts open for fear that the lifesaving wood will not be there when they need it. It was a trust among the outdoorspeople, we will keep our doors open; provided you uphold that sacred trust among neighbors and strangers to honor the code and re-stock the woodpile. If enough folks don't restock the woodpile and take advantage, locked doors are sure to follow.*

> *The civil justice system is similar to that old outdoorsman code. The courts are open and available for all citizens who need them. The same principles apply. The idea of fair compensation is the same as taking just what you need, no more, no less. You jurors are fulfilling the second principle, which is that you are giving of your time to so that it can*

benefit someone else. You are leaving that spare item behind, which is your service. And that final principle is there is well. Just as wood is critical to the whole success of this hut system, and it doesn't work if the owner or next person enters the hut to find an empty wood pile; honesty, simple words under oath, is critical to the success and integrity of the civil system. This system allows a private citizen like the Plaintiff to hail a large company into court to seek fair compensation; and it needs to be here for all people. It requires only that they speak the truth and take their oath as a sacred trust. If people are not honest, if they try and take more than what they are entitled to, then it's really the same as not stocking the woodpile.

You are the judges of credibility in this case. There is no light on the witness box that tells you what is true or false. I would not presume to tell you what to believe or not believe. But I will ask you whether you think that the Plaintiff's witnesses upheld their end of their code. Did they treat this matter as a sacred trust with their fellow citizens that began at the dawn of our history and continues today to seek only fair compensation in a time of need? Did they treat their oath to tell the truth with the same respect that an outdoorsman treated his sacred obligation to replace the wood that he used? I leave that determination to you.

Then, I will usually refer to specific portions of a transcript where what they said did not turn out to be true, with the same open ended question. Does this suggest that the Plaintiff respected his oath as a sacred trust with his fellow citizens; or that he is the type of person to see an unlocked hut door, and just see an individual opportunity?

Even among urban jurors, there is some appeal to this old argument. There is a lot unsaid. The idea is that we don't leave our doors open anymore because folks took advantage of others good nature; and the civil justice system is just as fragile if greedy folks like the Plaintiff try and get over, then it's not going to be there for you when you need it. In its simplest form, it is a version of a golden rule argument so it's very very close to the line. I don't use it as frequently now as I used to because there was a time it hit the judges in my area and more than one of them would say to me, "I don't want to hear any of that woodpile argument." Like I said, it's very close to the line, and I wouldn't want to have a verdict undone because I pushed the closing to the edge. I still push a lot of the same themes without the wood pile metaphor.

Last, it's easy to get lost when speaking, especially in a closing, so Master Trial Attorney's have a rehearsed "final five minutes" that they generally use in each case to sum it up and bring them home when they lose themselves in their own thoughts. It may be as simple as "Thank you for your time. My job is done, but the most important job has just begun, and that is your job, to evaluate what you have heard and make a decision in this case."

*****

EPILOGUE
The Killing of Billy Holley

I once asked my Dad if he would defend someone guilty of murder. It was an innocent question from a kid worried that his Dad might be one of those seedy lawyers everyone hated, one who would get guilty people off on technicalities if you paid him enough money to do it. What began with a kid wanting assurance his Dad was good left him years later looking into his own heart, as that kid turned lawyer sat in a courtroom defending a man charged with murder.

"Dad, would you defend someone guilty of murder?"

"Well, if they are guilty, they've already been tried and convicted which means they don't need a lawyer."

It was a nice way of showing me that I was the one who was guilty - guilty of not being fair, but I was trying to learn and his kind, patient tone showed he understood.

"Well, what if he told you he did it, before he got tried, would you defend him?"

"Well, why did he do it?"

"What do you mean?"

"What was his reason for killing, that's important to know don't you think?"

He knew what I meant. I didn't mean a justified killing. Why my Dad made simple questions so difficult I never understood. But, this was a lesson that words having meaning, and meaning makes all the difference to the question being asked, and justice demanded the right question be asked to get a just answer.

"Well Dad, what if he didn't have any reason, what if he just robbed a store and killed someone?"

I asked this because not long before, my Dad represented the estate of a young grocery clerk killed in a store robbery, killed by an escaped prisoner. It was a case that pained my Dad, because the "estate" was a loving young wife and baby boy left fatherless.

"So, do we kill all people who kill someone else? What if someone killed because they were driving drunk, crashed, and another drunk person in their car died. They didn't intend to kill their friend but did. Do we kill that person because they killed their friend?"

I hadn't thought about that, and he saw in my eyes that I hadn't.

"You see son, we are here to make sure a person gets a fair trial, make sure we know what happened, why it happened, and if someone did wrong, make sure that the punishment fits the crime, meaning the punishment has to be just and fair."

I thought often about our conversation, and found myself thinking about it during the trial of John Holley, accused of murdering his brother Billy. I was defending John. It was my first murder trial. As I waited for the prosecutor to finish his unbearably long closing argument, so that I could make mine, my Dad's words "what is just and fair" reverberated through my mind. The prosecutor said John was guilty. I was getting ready to argue that he wasn't, at least not as guilty as the prosecutor said he was. I had to concede some guilt because the judge wouldn't let me argue self-defense.

How much time John would do in prison now hinged on the semantics of whether the killing was 1st degree murder, 2nd degree murder, or manslaughter. When you read the definitions of them, there wasn't a lot of articulable difference between them, thus the tone of voice and emphasis of facts used by the lawyers arguing for one or the other would make all the difference. If they believed the prosecutor, John would be guilty of 1st degree murder and spend up to the next forty years doing hard time; If it was 2nd degree murder, up to twenty years, and manslaughter, up to ten. John was going to do time, the only question was how long.

I wished my Dad was here to close it up, for he always had a way of succinctly saying things that made sense. But he wasn't here, and John sat next to me wondering what I would say. He was as sober and nervous as I was. I had written my closing down the night before and intended to follow it, but I can't say that I did, because when it was my turn to speak I left my notes on the table and talked to the jury, because I knew my Dad would do the same. I only hoped I could do it like he could.

John had stabbed his older brother Billy to death, I confessed, but not surprisingly, the two were drunk when it happened. They were always drunk, drinking and fighting in that little house. The only thing which was surprising was it wasn't John that died. By all accounts, Billy was older and meaner, and was a mean drunk, not a happy drunk and not a sleepy drunk, a mutual friend who was there testified to that. That mutual friend said Billy was a mean drunk, that John was not, and that the friend left because Billy was starting to get mean, and he knew what that meant, there was going to be a fight and he didn't want to be there when it happened, for Billy would be angry at anyone there.

After the friend left, Billy directed his anger at the only person left, his little brother John, and gave way to the usual bullying of his younger brother. That bullying turned into a fight in the kitchen when Billy attacked John in the kitchen.

John grabbed a small pocket knife, the kind you can buy at any local store, and poked it forward to keep Billy away from him. John poked Billy one time and poked him just above the belly-button. If Billy had any belly to him, it wouldn't have done a thing, probably wouldn't even have bled, but on Billy the point of that small blade went just deep enough to pierce his aorta.

The prosecutor would have you believe that John then coldly watched Billy bleed to death on the kitchen floor before he called an ambulance, and that warrants finding him guilty of 2nd degree murder, maybe worse, but that can't be true. How do we know it's not true? Because we know the time John called the ambulance and we know the time that the ambulance arrived. The ambulance arrived within five minutes only because they lived so close to the fire station. When the paramedics found Billy, they found he still had a pulse, which means Billy was still alive, he hadn't bled out as the prosecutor says. You also heard a doctor say that he would have bled out within five minutes, all of which means, John didn't coldly watch his brother bleed out before calling an ambulance. John called the ambulance right away.

There's nothing to suggest John intended, in any way, to kill his brother. Maybe he should have run out of the house that night or called the police, but he didn't but he also didn't intend to kill him either. He didn't stab more than once, and the wound was so small it's was barely visible. It was only a quick protective jab to keep his brother away, but unfortunately, it did more than that. When he realized what he had done, he called an ambulance, surrendered to the police, and always testified truthfully about what happened that night.

The reason you are instructed on the law of manslaughter, it because this was manslaughter, nothing more, convicting him of anything more would make this crime more than it was. It was two drunk brothers, and one of those brothers was mean drunk, but not John. John wasn't mean. Those words are not mine, but the words of a mutual friend. I ask that in passing sentence, you please insure you consider all the facts that night to determine which punishment is the proper judgment for this crime.

In the end, the jury returned a verdict of manslaughter. And I was done defending a guilty man. John went to jail and the lawyer who defended a man charged with murder, me, went home thinking about what his Father told him so many years before and wondering to himself always, was it just and fair? Did I do my job?

About the Author

Chris Lisle received his law degree from the University of Arkansas in 1993 and began practicing law with his Father. He has over Twenty years' trial experience handling complex litigation including construction defects, personal injury, criminal, contracts, real estate, and other matters and along the way created a bit of new law in the following reported decisions:

Mears v. Nationwide Mut. Ins. Co., 91 F.3d 1118 (C.A.8, Ark., 1996); *Shepherd v. Washington County*, 331 Ark 480, 962 SW 2d 779 (1998) Case of First Impression interpreting Arkansas Civil Rights Act; *Bedford v. Fox*, 333 Ark 509, 970 SW 2d 251 (1998) Case of First Impression under Arkansas Usury law; *Arkansas Democrat Gazette v. Zimmerman*, 341 Ark 771 (2000), Writ of Certiorari holding court's gag order was an abuse of discretion; *Brown v. Johnson*, 81 Ark App 60, 90 SW 30 924 (2003); Holding that an adopted child was excluded from a deed; *Mobley Law Firm P.A. v. Lisle Law Firm P.A.*, 353 Ark 828, 120 SW 3d 537 (2003), Holding client had "cause" for terminating attorney's services; *Benton County Stone, Inc. vs. Benton County Planning Board*, 374 Ark 519, 288 S.W.3d 653 (2008), decision upholding the denial of a re-zoning request.

After his father passed, he began managing litigation for a top "Fortune 50" company. He is a veteran of the US Army, having served in the 82nd Airborne Division. He completed Army Ranger School (awarded Ranger Tab, 1989); Army Parachute School, and German Parachute Wings. He enlisted after high school, was later commissioned in college, and honorably discharged as a Captain in the Infantry (USAR). He completed an Iron Distance Triathlon, Four Marathons, climbed Mt. Kilimanjaro in Africa, and has made fire without matches.

www.ingramcontent.com/pod-product-compliance
Lightning Source LLC
Chambersburg PA
CBHW070130240526
45468CB00002BA/848